D1567818

Drug Identification

Designer and Club Drugs
Quick Reference Guide

Detective Scott W. Perkins

Alliance Press

Printed in the United States of America.

ISBN: 1-890704-50-4
99-504

 **Alliance Press**

1527 Brighton Drive • Carrollton, TX 75007 • (800) 970-1883

Address all correspondence and order information to the above address.

Disclaimer

The function of the publisher is the distribution of the information contained in this text. It should be understood that by making this information available for educational purposes only, Alliance Press is in no manner or form endorsing, approving or advocating the use of any illegal substance or the abuse of any legal substance. Alliance Press is not responsible for the content or interpretation of this text. Alliance Press expressly disclaims any liability or responsibility for the misuse or abuse of any information contained herein. Alliance Press further expressly disclaims any liability or responsibility for any actual or consequential damages arising from such misuse or abuse, if any.

TABLE OF CONTENTS

INTRODUCTION

What Every Person Should Know

I first saw an MDMA (XTC) pill in 1991 at a Rave club in Orlando, Florida. Since that day, I have witnessed dozens of people experiencing seizures, blackouts, and trips to the emergency room for advanced life support due to various designer and club drugs they ingested at Rave parties. I have seen the philosophy of the Raves change from peace, love and togetherness to money, drugs and violence. Organized gang members use Rave clubs and parties to sell their heroin, GHB, crystal-meth and other deadly drugs. The drug dealers target misinformed people who believe they can safely take these drugs and have a good experience. Unfortunately, the potential drug user is not told how addicting and deadly the drugs can be, nor does he or she realize how devastating it is for parents to be called to the emergency room because their child has died from a drug overdose.

While working as an undercover detective in Rave clubs and within the Rave community, I gained firsthand insight as to how widespread and sophisticated the driving force is behind the drug distribution and Raves. The drug problem in the Raves initially started in the early '90s and has escalated to rapes, assaults, murders and other violent crimes. Civilian law enforcement, military police and intelligence, educators, and community leaders who believe that this problem does not exist in their communities are mistaken and most likely simply unaware of the indicators.

We are years behind in education and training on the various designer and club drugs. We must expand our knowledge in an effort to effectively enforce laws, educate our communities, and prevent more needless deaths.

This guide was originally designed as my personal reference manual while working undercover in the Raves and Rave communities. I was constantly confronted with designer and club drugs that were unfamiliar to me due to the lack of formal training available within law enforcement. After sustaining a gunshot wound during a successful hostage rescue in 1997, I had the time to dedicate to writing this formal reference guide. I hope that the material in this guide will assist you in performing your job as a law enforcement officer, educator, community leader and/or parent.

Raves and the Rave Subculture

RAVES
- All night dance parties designed to enhance an euphoric experience through music, drugs and dancing.
- The success of a Raves party is gauged on the disc jockey's performance and the quality of drugs available.

ORIGINATED IN EUROPE
- Mid '80s
- Attracted several thousand people
- Abundance of drug use
- Took place in both off-site locations and mainstream clubs
- Was aggressively policed by authorities

ATTRACTED AMERICANS (RAVE WAVE)
- Devoted Ravers 1990-91
- Believed in the Rave concept
- The drugs enhanced the music and the dance
- Promoted peace, not violence
- Raves were held in open-air areas and underground clubs
- Events attracted several thousand people
- Ravers that started during this time period are now called "old schoolers" or "old school Ravers"

RAVES TAKE ON A NEW MEANING
- Mid to late '90s
- Massive drug consumption
- Opportunity to make large sums of money
- Moved into mainstream clubs
- Organized gangs selling drugs

- Violence and criminal activity rose
    a. Robberies
    b. Home invasions
    c. Rapes
    d. Murders
- Increase in overdoses and deaths due to poly drug abuse
- Old School Ravers do not agree with the new wave and say they lost the concept behind it all . . . Peace, Love and Togetherness

PROBLEMS IN ORLANDO
- Raves being held in downtown clubs
- Start at 0300 until 0900
- Drug overdoses
    a. Clubs hire off-duty police and paramedics
- Organized drug distribution
    a. In clubs
    b. Off-site resupply areas
        1. Cars and hotel rooms
    c. Using security measures
        1. Runners
        2. Mediators
        3. Bodyguards
        4. Drug holder
        5. Money holder
        6. Commander
    d. Employing trained personnel
        1. Counter surveillance
        2. Background checks on undercover agents
        3. Enforcers/guards
        4. Looking for cops

5. Laws were taught to gang members
   a) Search and seizures
   b) Way to avoid detection
      1) Smuggling techniques
      2) Strict rules during drug distribution
1. Gang members attracted to Rave clubs
   a. Abundance of customers for their drug sales
   b. Rip-off other dealers
   c. Enjoy atmosphere
      1. Can party and sell drugs
2. Crimes escalated
   a. Property crimes
      1. Pay for drugs
      2. Support lifestyle
         a) Hard to keep jobs
   b. Home invasions
   c. Person robberies
      1. Steal drugs
      2. Steal money
   d. Rapes
      1. Opportunistic
      2. Sexual predators
- Orlando gained worldwide fame
   a. Rolling Stone Magazine
      1. Named Orlando techno capital of the world
   b. Rave promoters
   c. Record companies
   d. Internet
- Orlando Police Drug Enforcement
   a. Conducted two successful counter drug operations in Rave clubs
      1. Operation Rave '96
      2. Operation Rave '97

- City passes Rave ordinance
  a. Shuts down clubs at 0300
  b. Dispersed problem to unexpected areas
  c. Forced Raves back underground

RAVES ARE BIG BUSINESS
- Promoters (set up Raves throughout the U.S.)
  a. Open-air Raves
  b. Employ mobile set-up crew
     1. State-of-the-art equipment
     2. Advertisement techniques
     3. Difficult to track
  c. Pay $20,000 up front
  d. Brings in $100,000
     1. Per event
     2. Cash money
     3. Huge profit
- Cruise lines (ships)
  a. Raves on the sea
  b. Two-day party boat
- Airlines
  a. Offering service to annual Rave events in Europe, Australia and South Africa

RAVE EDUCATION BROADCAST
- January 21st and March 25th, 1998
- Several hundred thousand viewers
- Calls from rural areas stating they have problem with Raves

RAVERS
- 10 to 35 years of age
- All nationalities
- Majority are middle class

LOCATION OF RAVES
- Europe
- Australia
- South Africa
- America

LOCATIONS IN THE UNITED STATES
- Throughout the United States
- Promoters are starting to target rural communities that are not informed about Raves

TYPES OF RAVES
- Lawful
- Raves held in legitimate clubs
- Raves are open so the drug dealing is covert
- Participants will be older due to identification checks at the entrance

UNLAWFUL
- Non-licensed club or site
- Raves are covert so the drug dealing is more open
- Participants are younger

ADVERTISING TECHNIQUES
- Flyers
  a. Very professional
- Telephonic message
  a. Primary and secondary sites for Raves
- Underground record stores
- Word of mouth
- Internet

RAVE MUSIC
- Electronically produced
- 140 to 200 beats per minute
- Played by disc jockeys
  a. DJs have a very high status in the Rave community

b. Have a dedicated following of Ravers
- Psychedelic lights enhance the musical experience

TYPES OF MUSIC
- Techno
- Ambient
- Cosmic
- Jungle
- Happy hardcore
- House
- Old school

RAVE CLOTHING
- Baggies
- Baseball caps
- Acid/psychedelic
- Sports jerseys
- Cartoon characters on clothing
- Old soccer
- Stocking caps
- Beachwear

RAVE ACCESSORIES
- Silver jewelry
- Body piercing
  a. Eyebrows
  b. Belly button
  c. Nipples
  d. Tongue
  e. Ears
  f. Nose
  g. Lip

Schedules

The Controlled Substance Act is federal law and categorizes controlled substances into one of five schedules based on the drug's . . .
   a. potential for abuse
   b. physical and psychological dependence
   c. current accepted medical use in the United States

SCHEDULE I
   a. The drug or other substance has a high potential for abuse.
   b. The drug or other substance has no currently accepted medical use in treatment in the United States.
   c. There is a lack of accepted safety for use of the drug or other substance under medical supervision.

SCHEDULE II
   a. The drug or other substance has a high potential for abuse.
   b. The drug or other substance has a currently accepted medical use in treatment in the United States or a currently accepted medical use with severe restrictions.
   c. Abuse of the drug or other substances may lead to severe psychological or physical dependence.

SCHEDULE III
    a. The drug or other substance has a potential for abuse less than the drugs or other substances in Schedules I and II.

    b. The drug or other substance has a currently accepted medical use in treatment in the United States.

    c. Abuse of the drug or other substance may lead to moderate or low physical dependence or high psychological dependence.

SCHEDULE IV
    a. The drug or other substance has a low potential for abuse relative to the drugs or other substances in Schedule III.

    b. The drug or other substance has a currently accepted medical use in treatment in the United States.

    c. Abuse of the drug or other substance may lead to limited physical dependence or psychological dependence relative to the drugs or other substances in Schedule III.

SCHEDULE V
    a. The drug or other substance has a low potential for abuse relative to the drugs or other substances in Schedule IV.

    b. The drug or other substance has a currently accepted medical use in treatment in the United States.

    c. Abuse of the drug or other substance may lead to limited physical dependence or psychological dependence relative to the drugs or other substances in Schedule IV.

XTC Tablet
"Lightening Bolt"

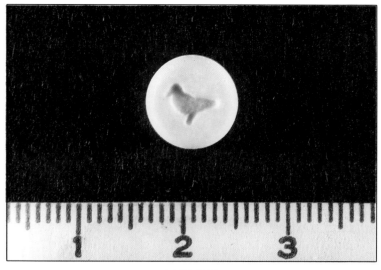

XTC Tablet
"Dove"

MDMA (Ecstasy)

MDMA
- Stands for 3,4-methlenedioxymethamphetamine
- Schedule I
- Central nervous system stimulant
- Synthetic drug produced in a clandestine laboratory
- Called the "love drug" and is the drug of choice at Rave clubs and parties

HISTORY
- MDMA was synthesized in the early 1900s
- Reviewed as a possible appetite suppressant but never marketed
- U.S. Army conducted studies of MDMA in the early 1950s
- MDMA was known as the "love drug" in the mid '70s
- Previously not a scheduled drug and sold openly
- Became the drug of choice in the wave of the Rave phenomenon in the early 1980s
- Classified as a "Schedule I" drug by the Drug Enforcement Administration in 1985

PRODUCTION OF MDMA
- MDMA Powder
  a. Manufactured in clandestine laboratories
  b. Varying degrees of purity levels
  c. Unqualified people combine and cook chemicals for human consumption
  d. Recipes for MDMA can be found on numerous internet sites
- Drug dealers who have access to MDMA powder . . .
  a. fill the gelatin capsules with MDMA and sell them at Rave clubs and parties

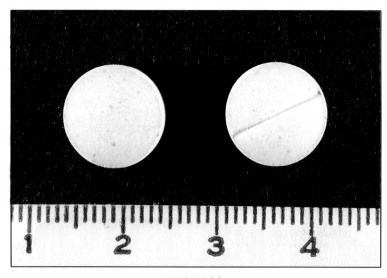

XTC Tablet
"Wafer"

b. compress the powder into tablet form giving the appearance of a legitimate and safe pill
   1. Requires a pill press and good binder
- The majority of the MDMA that is smuggled into the United States is already in tablet form

APPEARANCE
MDMA Powder
- Color varies from bright white to tan to brown
- Same texture as cocaine

MDMA Capsule
- Clear gelatin capsule
   a. Filled with MDMA powder
 - Small blue and white capsule
   a. Contain white MDMA powder
   b. Called "smurf"

MDMA Pill
- Size of an aspirin
- Varies in color
   a. Most common is off-white
- Has a design stamped on the front indicating name of pill
- May have a line scored on the back

MDMA "Bootleg" Pill
- Size of an aspirin
- Varies in color
- No markings on front or back

MDMA "Wafer"
- Size of a chewable vitamin "C"
- Off-white or tan in color with visible dark specks

PACKAGING
- Plastic ziplock baggie
- Shampoo bottle for overseas smuggling
- In packs of candies where its contents are the same size and consistency as the MDMA pill

XTC Tablet
"Double-Stack Roll"

XTC Tablet
"One Twenty Fives"

METHODS OF INGESTION/ONSET OF EFFECTS

- Orally   -   20 to 40 minutes
- Snorted (Powder)   -   5 to 10 minutes
- Smoked   -   20 to 30 seconds
- Injected   -   10 to 20 seconds

DURATION OF EFFECTS

- From 4 to 6 hours
- Hangover symptoms
    a. Last from 1 to 2 days
    b. Tired feeling
    c. Dullness of senses and mental process

DETECTION IN URINE

- Can be detected in urine from 2 to 5 days

PHYSICAL AND PSYCHOLOGICAL EFFECTS

Moderate Doses

- Euphoria   -   Hyperexcitability
- Nervousness   -   Rapid heartbeat

High Doses/Overdoses

- Teeth grinding   -   Eye twitching
- Scratching or rubbing skin -   Panic attacks
- Dizziness   -   Muscle cramping
- Loss of consciousness   -   Seizures

Dangers in Rave Clubs

- While using MDMA, a person may
    a. engage in exhausting physical activities (nonstop dancing)
    b. ignore physical injuries
    c. ignore the body's need for water and become dehydrated
    d. suffer heat strokes

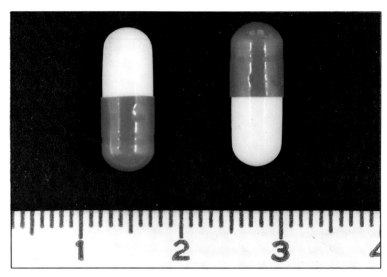

XTC Capsule
"Smurfs"

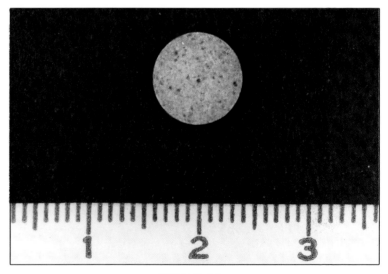

XTC Tablet
"Bootleg"

Physical and psychological dependence is unknown.
Tolerance can occur.

SIGNS AND SYMPTOMS OF A USER
Abundance of Energy
- Constant movements
- Free flowing conversations
- Sweating and deep breathing
- Scattered thought processing

Physical Touching
- Hugging each other
- Body massaging intensifies the high
- Rubbing different textures heightens sense of touch
- Aggressive sexual behavior through dancing and flirting

Involuntary Physical Reaction to MDMA
- Teeth grinding
- Biting lips and inner mouth
- Scratching and rubbing skin
- Jaw thrusting

SLANG TERMS AND STREET NAMES
- Rolls
- Pills
- Beans
- "X"

Terms indicating you are under the influence of MDMA
- Rolling
- Peaking
- Blowing up
- "X" ing

PARAPHERNALIA
- Blow pops and baby pacifiers used to keep MDMA users from grinding their teeth and biting their mouth
- Nasal inhalers and decongestant rubs
  a. Number 1 indicator of MDMA use

XTC Capsule
"Smurf" and the powder contained in it

XTC Capsule
"Quarter Cap," with the powder it contains

b. While under the influence of MDMA, the user enjoys the sensation of the menthol vapors passing through their body
c. Users will blow the vapors into each other's eyes for pleasure
d. The rub is placed on the upper lip to allow the vapors to be inhaled while dancing
- Surgical mask
   a. Menthol rub is spread inside the mask and passed around the dance floor allowing several MDMA users to inhale and enjoy the vapors
- Caffeine pills
   a. When MDMA users cannot get their supply, they will use caffeine pills to mimic the MDMA high

PRICES
- $20 to $25 per pill
- $200 to $250 per 10 pack
- Price negotiable for 100 pack
- Purchased in increments of 10, 20 or 50 pack

Rear View of a "Ruffie"

Flunitrazepam (Rohypnol®)

RUFFIES
- Street name for flunitrazepam (Rohypnol®)
- Schedule I
- Central nervous system depressant
- Ten times more powerful than Valium
- Not legally available in the United States

HISTORY
- Used in several foreign countries as a pre-surgical sedative and for the treatment of severe sleep disorders
- Some doctors in foreign countries administer flunitrazepam (Rohypnol®)to psychiatric patients
- First documented as an abused drug in the United States in the early '90s
- Gained national attention as a "date rape" drug

PRODUCTION OF FLUNITRAZEPAM (ROHYPNOL®)
- Chemical analog of diazepam
- Marketed by Roche Pharmaceuticals
- Legally available in Mexico, Europe, South America and Asia

APPEARANCE
- White-colored tablets
- Single or doublecross scored line on the back of tablet
- R.H., Roche or Ruffies on front of tablet
- The #1 or #2 scored on front of tablet indicating milligrams

When dissolved in a drink, flunitrazepam (Rohypnol®)is odorless and tasteless.

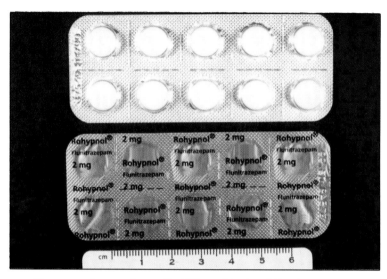

Front and rear view of a Blister Pack of flunitrazepam
(Rohypnol®)

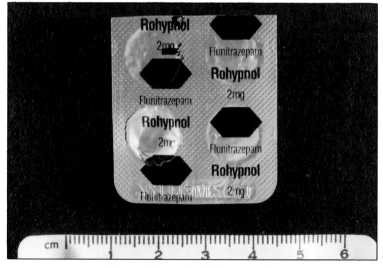

Rear view of a Blister Pack

PACKAGING
- Wrapped in bubble pack with clear front and silver peel-away backing with Roche and the number of milligrams written on it

METHODS OF INGESTION
- Swallowed
- Inhaled (crushed into powder)
- Injected
- Smoked (in Central Florida generally by Ravers)
- Dissolved in drink

DURATION OF EFFECTS
- Onset/15 to 20 minutes
- Peak/1 to 2 hours
- Duration/8 hours
- Hangover/12 to 24 hours

DETECTION IN URINE
- Standard drug testing may not detect flunitrazepam
- An advanced test targeting flunitrazepam is available

PHYSICAL AND PSYCHOLOGICAL EFFECTS
Moderate Doses
- Loss of inhibition
- Drunken state
- Dizziness
- Tranquility
- Slurred speech

High Doses/Overdoses
- Slowed breathing
- Headaches
- Affects judgement
- Memory loss
- Death
- Confusion
- Hallucinations
- Blackouts
- Comas

Physical and psychological dependence can occur.

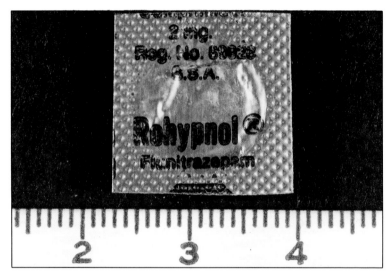

"Ruffies"

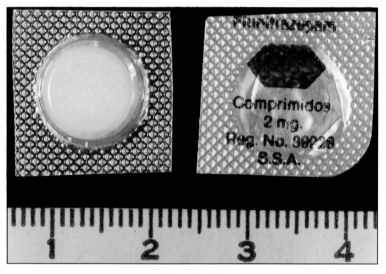

"Ruffies"

WITHDRAWAL SYMPTOMS
- Headaches
- Tension
- Irritability
- Hallucinations
- Muscle aches
- Confusion
- Delirium
- Convulsions

SLANG TERMS AND STREET NAMES
- Ruffie
- Dulcita
- Wheel
- "R-2"
- Shay
- Roach 2
- Landing gear
- Mind eraser

PRICES
- $5 to $25 per tablet in Rave clubs

Prices have escalated due to strict sentencing guidelines recently passed by the Federal Government. Dealers have raised their prices to compensate for the increased risk factors involved in selling flunitrazepam (Rohypnol®).

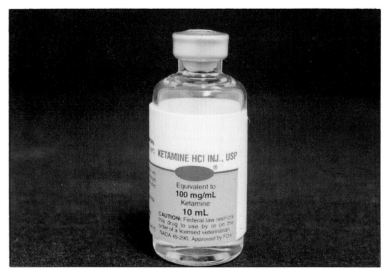

Ketamine in liquid form. One bottle can produce
approximately one gram of ketamine powder.

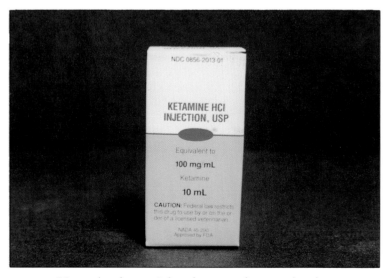

Ketamine box. A bottle costs the veterinarian
approximately six dollars.

Ketamine

KETAMINE
- Controlled substance in some states
- Classified as a disassociate anesthetic
- Closely related to PCP
- Has been abused since the early '70 s

HISTORY
- Developed in the early '60 s
- Used as an anesthetic during the Vietnam War
- Currently used as an anesthetic for animals
- Became a drug of choice at Rave parties during the mid-'90 s

PRODUCTION OF KETAMINE
- Ketamine HCL is manufactured in liquid form
- Brand names are Ketaset, Ketalar, Vetalar and Ketajet
- Drug dealers convert liquid ketamine into powder form via an evaporation method utilizing a microwave or oven

APPEARANCE
Liquid Form
- Clear
- Contained in 10 milliliter glass vial
- Glass vial will have ketamine written on it
Powder Form
- White in color
- Powder-like texture
- Close resemblance to cocaine

There is no current field test for ketamine. Specimens must be submitted to a laboratory for testing.

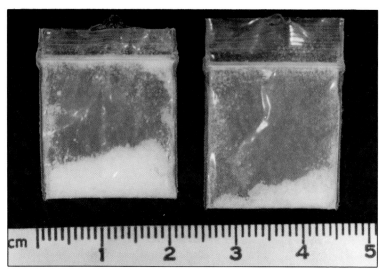

Ketamine powder in baggies.

Ketamine powder is inhaled with cut-off straws.

PACKAGING
Liquid Form
- Glass vial from Veterinary Hospital

Powder Form
- Small plastic baggie
- Tin foil
- One-hit bullet
- Capsule

METHODS OF INGESTION/ONSET OF EFFECTS
- Inhaled
- Injected
- Swallowed
- Smoked

- 5 to 10 minutes
- 1 to 2 minutes
- 15 to 20 minutes
- 2 to 5 minutes

DURATION OF EFFECTS
- 20 to 30 minutes
- Residual effects may be felt up to an hour after initial dose

Called the "Businessman's LSD" due to the short duration of the high.

PHYSICAL AND PSYCHOLOGICAL EFFECTS
Moderate Doses
- Euphoria
- Quick burst of energy
- Drunken feeling

- Loss of Inhibition
- Confusion
- Ringing in ears

High Doses/Overdoses
- Tunnel vision
- Shortness of breath
- Loss of balance
- Floating sensation
- Out-of-body experience
- Vomiting (when mixed with alcohol)

- Numbness of body
- Mental depression
- No sense of time
- Seizures
- Coma

Ketamine

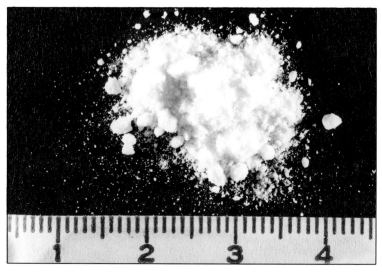

Ketamine powder has the same appearance as cocaine but is more "fluffy."

Physical and psychological dependence is possible. Tolerance can occur.

SLANG TERMS AND STREET NAMES
- Special K
- "K"
- Kat
- "K" wave
- "K" hole
- "K" head

PARAPHERNALIA
- Glass vials
- Hypodermic needles
- Plastic baggies
- Cut-off straws
- Lighters
- Razors

PRICES
- $6 to $8 per vial of Ketamine (legally obtained)
- $50 to $100 for a vial of Ketamine (illegally obtained)
- $20 for 0.2 grams of powder Ketamine

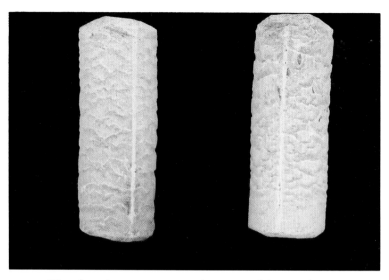

Heroin tubes, compressed, wrapped in condoms,
swallowed, and smuggled into the U.S.

Pieces of heroin broken from compressed tubes (very high
purity levels)

Heroin

HEROIN
- Schedule I
- Classified as a semi-synthetic narcotic
- Affects the central nervous system and acts as both a depressant and an analgesic (pain killer)

HISTORY
- Heroin was isolated from morphine in 1874
- It was thought to be the cure for morphine addiction
- Quickly addicted its users and became a problem drug
- In 1914 the Harrison Narcotic Act banned the importation of Heroin into the United States

PRODUCTION OF HEROIN
- The poppy plant, papaver somniferum, is grown throughout the world and produces opium
- Opium is processed producing morphine
- Morphine is synthesized producing Heroin
- Suppliers of Heroin to the United States
    a. Asia
    b. Mexico
    c. Columbia
        1. Primary source
        2. Highest purity levels of Heroin (60-85% pure)

APPEARANCE
- White powder
- Tan powder
- Black tar
- Tan colored tubes (3" long)
    a. Compressed Heroin powder is wrapped in condoms which are swallowed by humans and then smuggled in the United States

Heroin being ground into powder form.

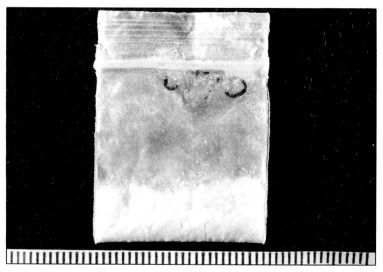

Heroin powder in small plastic baggie.

PACKAGING
- Tin foil
- Plastic baggie
- Capsule
- Balloons

METHODS OF INGESTION/ONSET OF EFFECTS
- Inhaled	1 to 3 minutes
- Smoked	20 to 30 seconds
- Injected	10 to 20 seconds
- Orally	Varies

DURATION OF THE EFFECTS
- 3 to 6 hours

DETECTION IN URINE
- From 1 to 4 days

PHYSICAL AND PSYCHOLOGICAL EFFECTS
Moderate Doses
- Euphoria
- Dreamy
- Warm "rush" sensation
- Constricted pupils
- Nausea

High Doses/Overdoses
- Restlessness
- Constipation
- Droopy eyelids
- Slow breathing
- Depressed cough reflux
- Death
- Sweatiness
- Lethargic
- Slow heart rate
- Sedation
- Respiratory failure

Physical and psychological dependence is possible. Tolerance can occur.

Heroin wrapped in small pieces of tin-foil called "Bindles"
or "Bags" cost approximately ten to twelve dollars.

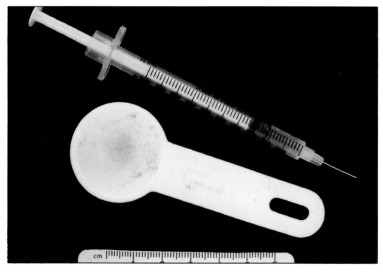

Heroin shoot-up kit.

WITHDRAWAL SYMPTOMS
- Insomnia
- Hot and cold flashes
- Nausea
- Vomiting
- Weakness
- Abdominal cramps
- Diarrhea

SIGNS OF HEROIN ABUSE
- Reduced energy level
- Lack of motivation
- Low sex drive
- Nodding out (falling asleep)
- Pinpointed pupils
- Long sleeve shirts worn during hot weather
- Blood stains on shirt sleeves
- Dry skin
- Watery eyes
- Cigarette burns on clothing, hands and furniture

SLANG TERMS AND STREET NAMES
- Smack
- Junk
- Bindles
- Bags
- Black tar
- Manteca
- Horse
- Bundles
- Tar

PARAPHERNALIA
- Hypodermic needles
- Lighters
- Tin foil
- Straws
- Aluminum bottle caps (cooking Heroin before injecting)
- Spoons
- Tourniquets
- Razors
- Mirrors
- Plastic baggies

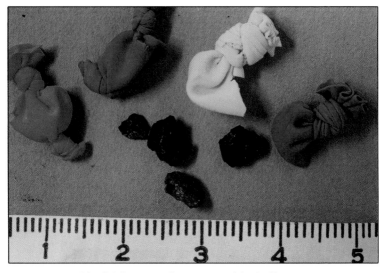

Black Tar Heroin wrapped in balloons.

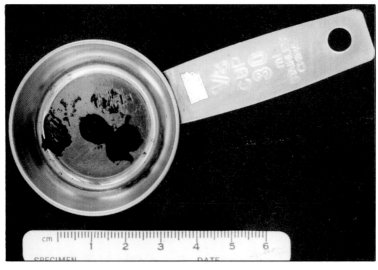

Black Tar Heroin.

<u>Heroin can be cut (adds volume) with:</u>
- Milk sugar
- Manitol
- Quinine
- Lactose
- Starch

PRICES
- $10 to $15 per dose (.2 to .4 grams)

In Central Florida, 1 gram costs from $100 to $150

GHB in squeeze bottle. GHB will form bubbles when shaken.

GHB

GHB
- Stands for **G**ama **H**ydroxy **B**utyrate
- Controlled substance in some states
- Central nervous system depressant
- Causes euphoria, hallucinations and deep sleep
- Called the "date rape" drug of the '90s

HISTORY
- Synthesized in 1961
- Developed for use as an anesthetic
- Used as a treatment for sleep disorders
- Aided in the treatment of alcoholism
- Used by bodybuilders as a growth hormone stimulant
- Banned by the Food and Drug Administration in 1990 due to several acute poisonings

PRODUCTION OF GHB
- Legally produced in Europe
  a. Legitimate laboratories
  b. Good quality control of product
  c. Accurate dosing levels
  d. Qualified chemist

- Illegally produced in the United States
  a. Made in kitchen laboratories
  b. Unstable quality of product
  c. Inaccurate dosing levels
  d. Local drug dealer acts as chemist

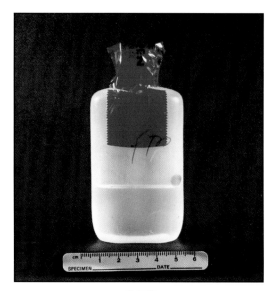

GHB

GHB in vial

The two main ingredients in GHB manufactured in the United States:
1. Industrial engine degreaser
2. Caustic acid

INTERNET CONNECTIONS
- Information available on producing GHB
- Home-cooking kits can be ordered for GHB production
- Offers safety tips on consuming GHB

APPEARANCE
Clear Liquid
- Odorless
- Salty taste
- Slightly thicker than water

White Powder Form
- Similar to powder cocaine

Attempts to Avoid Detection
- Adding artificial flavoring and coloring GHB
- Mixing GHB in bottled water and drinks that have a salty taste

PACKAGING
- Tin foil
- Plastic baggie
- Kid's "bubbles" jar
- Capsule
- Water bottle
- 35mm film canister

METHODS OF INGESTION
- Inhaled
- Injected
- Swallowed

35mm film canisters are used to carry GHB. The lid is used as the measuring cup for each $10.00 dose.

Bubble bottles are used to transport GHB due to the GHB having the same appearance as the bubbles (some liquid GHB will bubble when shaken).

EFFECTS OF GHB
- Onset 10 to 20 minutes
- Duration 1 to 3 hours
- After effects 2 to 4 hours

INTERNET RECOMMENDED DOSING LEVELS
- Low doses   .5 to 1.5 grams
- Moderate doses   1 to 3 grams
- High doses   3 to 8 grams

TESTING FOR GHB
In Humans
- Routine drug screen will not detect GHB
- You must request a test that specifically targets GHB
- GHB can be detected in both blood and urine
- Urine testing should be used since GHB leaves the bloodstream within 4 to 7 hours after consumption

Field Testing
- There is no specific field test for GHB
- Specimen must be sent to laboratory for testing

PHYSICAL AND PSYCHOLOGICAL EFFECTS
Low Doses
- Euphoria
- Anxiety
- Increased sexual pleasure
- Impaired judgement
- Loss of inhibition
- Loss of coordination
- Nausea

High Doses/Overdoses
- Dizziness
- Slowed breathing/heart rate
- Memory loss
- Respiratory depression
- Muscular fatigue
- Passing out
- Coma
- Death

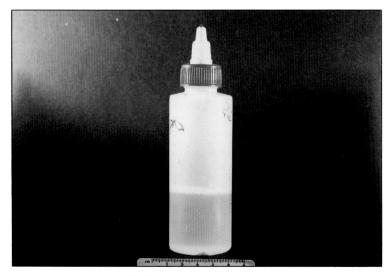

GHB in a squeeze bottle.

Water bottles are used to smuggle and consume GHB.

WITHDRAWAL SYMPTOMS
- Insomnia
- Anxiety
- Tremors
- Depression

SLANG TERMS AND STREET NAMES
- Liquid "E"
- Georgia homeboy
- Scoop
- Grievous bodily harm
- Liquid "X"
- "G"
- Easy lay
- Gamma 10
- Salty water

PARAPHERNALIA
- Water bottles
- Flavored food coloring
- 35mm film canisters
- Cut-off straws

PRICES
- $10 per dose (1/2 teaspoon) in Rave clubs

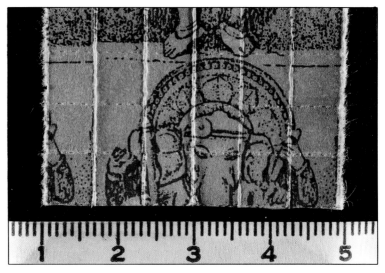

LSD blotter paper.

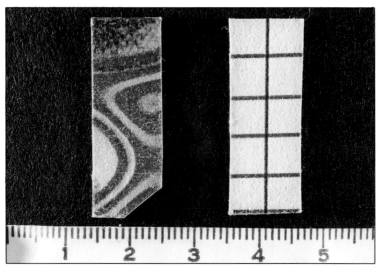

LSD blotter paper.

LSD

LSD
- Stands for Lysergic Acid Diethylamide
- Classified as a hallucinogen
- Semisynthetic drug manufactured in clandestine laboratories

HISTORY
- LSD was synthesized in 1938 in Switzerland
- It was developed as a circulatory and respiratory stimulant
- Controlled Substance Act of 1970 classified LSD as a Schedule I drug
- At the present time, LSD is abused throughout the United States

PRODUCTION OF LSD
Manufactured in Clandestine Laboratories
- The process involves the use of dangerous chemicals
LSD Clandestine Laboratories
- Located in California
- Very few in number
- Do not operate on a continual basis
  a. One week's worth of work can produce several months' supply of LSD

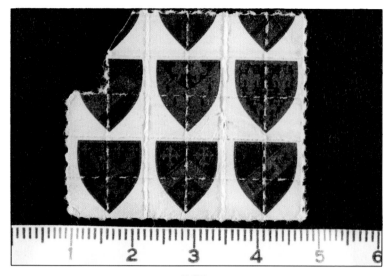

LSD

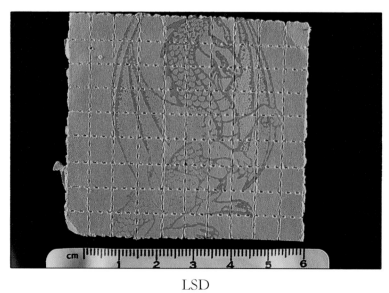

LSD

APPEARANCE
Pure LSD
- Clear or white
- Odorless and tasteless
- Crystalline material

Tablet form
- Microdots

Thin squares of gelatin
- Window panes

Sheets of perforated paper
- Blotter paper
- Covered with colorful designs
- Soaked in LSD

PACKAGING
- Plastic film canister
- Tin foil
- Plastic baggie
- Pack of gum

One hit (piece of blotter paper) is placed on an unwrapped stick of gum. The gum is re-wrapped and placed back into pack.

METHODS OF INGESTION/ONSET OF EFFECTS
- Orally
- 30 to 90 minutes

Average dose of LSD is 50 micrograms.

DURATION OF EFFECTS
- Approximately 12 hours

DETECTION IN URINE
Low doses
- 8 hours

High doses
- 30 hours

One piece of LSD worth 5-10 dollars.

PHYSICAL AND PSYCHOLOGICAL EFFECTS
- Depends on the user's mood, expectations, surroundings and dosing levels

Moderate Doses
- Dilated pupils
- Rapid change in emotions
- Decreased body temperature

- Rapid heart rate

High Doses/Overdoses
- Visual hallucination
- Distortion of sizes and shapes

- Impaired judgement

Users state they "hear colors" and "see sounds."

There is no physical dependence. Psychological dependence is unknown and tolerance can occur.

SLANG TERMS AND STREET NAMES
- Acid
- Double dome
- Sid
- Stamps
- A-bombs

- Paper
- Dots
- Blotter
- Trips
- Doses

PRICES
- Dose
- Sheet
- Book

- $5 to $10
- $150 to $200
- $900 to $1,000

Cocaine Hydrochloride
"Powder Coke"

Crack Cocaine

Cocaine

COCAINE
- Schedule II
- Central nervous system stimulant
- Most potent stimulant of natural origin
- High potential for abuse

HISTORY
- Initially used as an anesthetic in the late 1800s
- Aided in the treatment of asthma
- Previously an active ingredient in many soft drinks and teas
- Due to its abuse and adverse effects on addicts, its use was restricted in 1906

PRODUCTION OF COCAINE
- Extracted from the leaves of the erythroxylon coca bush
- Grows primarily in Peru and Bolivia
- Extracted through a chemical process involving . . .
  - a. sulfuric acid
  - b. acetone
  - c. potassium permanganate
  - d. hydrochloric acid
  - e. kerosene
  - f. gasoline

This process yields cocaine hydrochloride (cocaine powder).

PRODUCTION OF CRACK COCAINE
- Produced from cocaine hydrochloride through a heating and cooling process

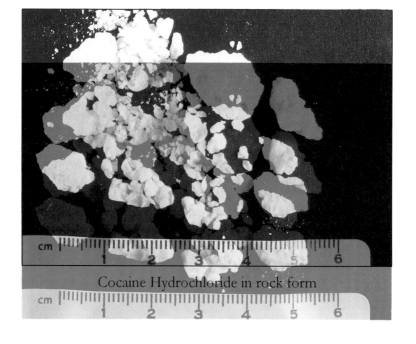

Cocaine Hydrochloride in rock form

A cocaine grinder, used to make cocaine powder

APPEARANCE
Powder Cocaine (Hydrochloride)
- White to off white in color
- Powder
- Flaky
- Rock (not crack/compressed powder)

1. Cocaine hydrochloride in rock form usually indicates that it has recently been cut from a kilo brick of cocaine and that the purity level is very high.

2. There is a system called "re-rocking" cocaine. Dealers will add cut to the cocaine expanding the volume and decreasing the purity level. They will compress the powder back into rock form enabling them to sell it at higher prices as "uncut" cocaine.

Crack Cocaine
- White to tan in color
- Rock-like substance
- Waxy appearance

PACKAGING
- Clear plastic baggie
- Glass vial
- Tin foil
- Kilo bricks wrapped in tape
- Street-level dealers of crack . . .
    a. hold loose pieces in their mouths and hands for easy disposal
    b. hide plastic baggies in tongues of tennis shoes and front flap opening of male underwear

Crack Cocaine.
Two sugar cookies; both approximately one ounce of crack.

Pieces of crack cocaine.

METHODS OF INGESTION/ONSET OF EFFECTS
- Inhaled
- Injected
- Orally
- Smoked

- 3 to 5 minutes
- 5 to 10 seconds
- 3 to 5 minutes
- 5 to 10 seconds

DURATION OF EFFECTS
- From 1 to 2 hours

DETECTION IN URINE
- From 2 to 4 days

PHYSICAL AND PSYCHOLOGICAL EFFECTS
Moderate Doses
- Increased alertness
- Euphoria
- Loss of appetite

- High blood pressure
- Increased heart rate
- Dilated pupils

High Doses/Overdoses
- Agitation
- Confusion
- Hallucinations
- Cardiac arrest

- Panic attacks
- Paranoia
- Convulsions

Physical dependence is possible. Psychological dependence is high. Tolerance can occur.

WITHDRAWAL SYMPTOMS
- Irritability
- Sluggishness
- Prolonged period of sleep

- Depression
- Nausea

Crack cocaine paraphernalia.

Cocaine powder paraphernalia. The vice and the pipe are used for the re-rocking of powder cocaine.

SLANG TERMS AND STREET NAMES
- Blow
- Hard
- Flake
- Coke
- Base
- White
- Powder
- Dime
- Rock

PARAPHERNALIA
Cocaine Powder
- Straws
- Mirrors
- Razor blades
- Grinders
- Spoons
- Plastic baggies
- Scales

Cocaine powder can be cut with lactose, manitol, inositol, and lidocane.

Crack Cocaine
- Lighters
- Tin cans (crack pipe)
- Glass tubes (crack pipe)
- Antennas (crack pipe)
- Brillo pads
- Razor blades
- Thin wipers

PRICES
Cocaine Powder
- $80 to $100 per gram
Crack Cocaine
- $10 to $20 per 0.2 grams
- Small rock ($10)
- Medium size block ($50)
- Sugar cookie ($900)

Prices vary throughout the United States for larger quantities of cocaine.

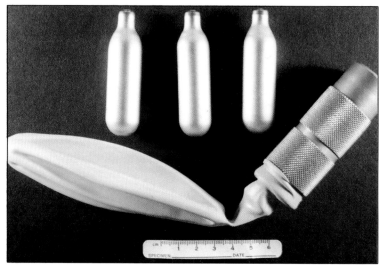

Balloons are filled with mind-altering gases.

Inhalants

INHALANTS
- Consist of common household and workplace products
- Affect the central nervous system
- Can cause Sudden Sniffing Death (SSD)

CATEGORIES OF INHALANTS
- Volatile solvents
- Aerosols
- Anesthetics
- Nitrates
  a. Amyl nitrate
  b. Butyl nitrate

EXAMPLES OF INHALANTS
- Airplane glue
- Rubber cements
- Nail polish remover
- Spray paint
- Whipped cream cans
- Correction fluid
- Gasoline
- Nitrous oxide
- Paint thinner
- Air freshener

METHODS OF INGESTION
- Inhaling fumes through the nose
- Breathing fumes into the mouth
- Consuming fumes through the nose and mouth simultaneously

TECHNIQUES OF INGESTION
- Sniffing directly from container
- Breathing through a rag soaked in the mind-altering chemicals
- Breathing from a plastic bag containing a chemically soaked rag

Whipped cream canister.

Spray paint and paint thinner are commonly used as an inhalant.

-   Breathing directly from cylinders or balloons containing mind-altering gases

DANGERS ASSOCIATED WITH INHALANTS

-   Asphyxia
-   Cardiac arrest
-   Loss of consciousness
-   Sudden Sniffing Death
-   Suffocation
-   Choking on vomit

DURATION OF EFFECTS

-   Onset   2 to 4 seconds
-   Duration of high   1 to 2 minutes

PHYSICAL AND PSYCHOLOGICAL EFFECTS

Immediate

-   Alcohol-like intoxication
-   Loss of coordination
-   Double vision
-   Headache
-   Ringing in ears
-   Chest pains
-   Anxiety
-   Confusion
-   Nausea

Long Term

-   Tremors
-   Weight loss
-   Impaired respiratory system
-   Lack of concentration
-   Damage to central nervous system
-   Cardiac arrest
-   Irritation to nose and mouth
-   Death

Physical and psychological dependence is possible. Tolerance can occur.

Nitrous oxide tank rigged with soda bottles and tubes to allow two people to get high at the same time.

Correction fluid.

WITHDRAWAL SYMPTOMS
- Hallucination
- Headache
- Nausea
- Chills
- Tremors

SIGNS OF INHALANTS ABUSE
- Red and glassy eyes
- Dilated pupils
- Very moody
- Drastic change in appearance
- Poor hygiene
- Loss of appetite
- Lack of concentration
- Scattered thought process
- Chemical odor on clothes or in room
- Inflamed nose or nosebleeds
- Rash or sores around nose and lips

SLANG TERMS AND STREET NAMES
- Whippets
- Ozone
- Thrust
- Poppers
- Climax
- Rush
- Locker room
- Nitrous
- Canisters

PARAPHERNALIA
- Balloons
- Rags
- Plastic bags
- Nitrous tanks and canisters
- Gas cans
- Paint cans
- Empty glue bottles

PRICES
- Balloons filled with nitrous sell for $2
- Inhalants are purchased in stores at the current selling price

Two marijuana "buds"

Marijuana stems and seeds

Marijuana

MARIJUANA
- Schedule I
- Comes from the plant cannabis sativa
- Contains the psychoactive ingredient THC (delta-9-tetrahydrocannabinol)
- Abused throughout the United States

HISTORY
- The plant cannabis sativa grows wildly in most of the tropical regions of the world
- Marijuana was readily available and used in the United States during the early 1900s
- Attempts to regulate and tax the drug took place in 1937
- The Controlled Substance Act of 1970 classified marijuana as a Schedule I drug

APPEARANCE
Marijuana (The Plant)
- Green, leafy bush
- Varying height (2 to 10 feet)
- Very distinctive leaves
    a. Usually have odd number of strands
    b. Strands of the leaf are serrated

On the Street (Mixture)
- Buds
- Leaves
- Seeds
- Color may range from bright to dull green or brown
- Marijuana wrapped in white rolling paper is called a joint
- Marijuana wrapped in a cigar is called a blunt

Marijuana wrapped in cigarette paper, called a "joint."

Marijuana wrapped in cigar paper, called a "blunt."

PACKAGING
-   Plastic baggie
-   35mm film container
-   Garbage bag
-   Wrapped in plastic to avoid odor
-   One or two pounds compressed bricks have been wrapped in plastic then covered with plaster to avoid odor

METHODS OF INGESTION/ONSET OF EFFECTS
-   Smoked
-   10 to 30 minutes
-   Orally
-   Varies

DURATION OF EFFECTS
-   From 2 to 3 hours

DETECTION IN URINE
-   Up to 30 days

PHYSICAL AND PSYCHOLOGICAL EFFECTS
Moderate Doses
-   Relaxation
-   Euphoria
-   Happiness
-   Increased heart rate
-   Impaired short-term

High Doses/Overdoses
-   Paranoia
-   Restlessness
-   Increased appetite
-   Anxiety attacks
-   Impaired coordination
-   Panic attacks
-   Altered perception

Physical dependence is unknown. Psychological dependence and tolerance are possible.

Two "dime bags," each worth ten dollars.

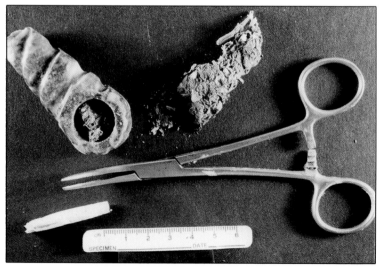
Marijuana and paraphernalia:
"Smoking bong" and forceps, which hold small joints.

WITHDRAWAL SYMPTOMS
- Insomnia
- Decreased appetite
- Nausea
- Irritability
- Anxieties

SLANG TERMS AND STREET NAMES
- Weed
- Pot
- "J"
- Herb
- Joint
- Blunt
- Kind
- Crippie

PARAPHERNALIA
- Bongs
- Rolling papers
- Roach clips
- Scales
- Lighters
- Large plate for cutting and removing seeds from marijuana
- Dug out
  a. Metal pipe with a hollow end that holds marijuana
- Aluminum foil pipes
- Aluminum cans for smoking marijuana

PRICES
- $10 for a dime bag (2 to 3 grams)
- $100 to $300 per ounce

Methamphetamine rock and powder.

Two small meth-rocks.

Methamphetamine

METHAMPHETAMINE
- Schedule II
- An amphetamine analog
- Central nervous system stimulant
- Triggers the release of large amounts of dopamine norepinephrine in the brain
- High potential for abuse
- Prolongs person's ability to perform their duties

HISTORY
1930's-1950's
- Primary ingredient in the Benzedrine inhaler
- Treatment for narcolepsy
- Used to keep soldiers alert during combat

1960's-Present
- Produced in clandestine laboratories
- Used as a party drug
- Abused throughout the United States
- Presently a national problem affecting both large cities and rural America

PRODUCTION OF METHAMPHETAMINE
- Clandestine laboratories
  Consideration for Selecting Lab Sites
    a. Access to power source
    b. Area that offers privacy
    c. Good ventilation
    d. Sufficient cooking space
    e. Ability to dispose of chemical waste

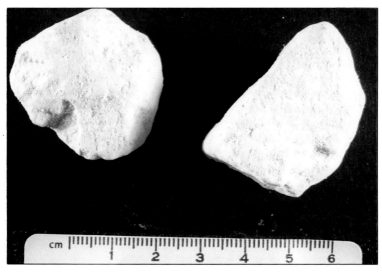

Two large meth-rocks, will be crushed into powder.

Meth-powder.

- Clandestine laboratories (continued)
  Dangers Associated with Clandestine Labs
  a. Chemicals used to produce the drug
     1. Highly volatile
     2. Toxic
     3. Cause permanent damage to humans and the environment
  b. Security systems
     1. Attack dogs
     2. Booby-traps
     3. Armed guards
  Methods of Cooking Methamphetamine
  a. P2P method (Phenyl-2-Propanone)
  b. Ephedrine reduction
  c. Cold cook method
  Identifying a Clandestine Lab
  a. Generators supplying power
  b. Exhaust fans
  c. Chemical smell
  d. Boards on windows
  e. Chemical containers in yard
  f. Occupants up all night
  g. People stepping outside to smoke
- Desired product
  Methamphetamine (Hypochloride)
  a. Crank is a form of Methamphetamine that consists of tiny granular crystals that have the appearance of powder
  b. Ice is a form of Methamphetamine that consists of large crystals that have the appearance of rock candy

Methamphetamine.

Meth-powder.

APPEARANCE
- Crank
  a. Powder or compressed powder that gives the appearance of a rock (not Ice)
  b. Off-white or tan
  c. Off-white with a red tint
- Ice
  a. Clear rock
     The clear appearance indicates that it is water based and when smoked leave a white milky residue
  b. Yellowish rock
     The yellowish appearance indicates that it is oil based and when smoked leaves a black residue

  Ice is odorless and tasteless when smoked.

PACKAGING
- Tin foil
- Paper
- Glass vial
- Capsule
- Plastic baggie

METHODS OF INGESTION/ONSET OF EFFECTS
- Inhaled
- Injected
- Swallowed
- Smoked
- 3 to 5 minutes
- 5 to 10 minutes
- 15 to 20 minutes
- 5 to 10 minutes

DURATION OF THE HIGH
- From 4 to 8 hours

DETECTION IN URINE
- As soon as 1 hour after initial dose and up to 48 hours afterwards

Meth-powder in a one-hit bullet.

Meth-powder in small baggie.

PHYSICAL AND PSYCHOLOGICAL EFFECTS

<u>Moderate Doses</u>

- Euphoria
- Alertness
- Enhanced concentration
- Elevated blood pressure

- Loss of appetite
- Dilated pupils

<u>High Doses/Frequent Use</u>

- Malnutrition
- Physical burnout
- Aggressive behavior
- Stroke

- Rapid weight loss
- Paranoia
- Convulsion
- Death

Physical and psychological dependence is possible.
Tolerance can occur.

WITHDRAWAL SYMPTOMS

- Depression
- Nausea
- Severe craving for drugs

- Shaking
- Desire to sleep
- Loss of energy

SLANG TERMS AND STREET NAMES

- Batu
- Speed
- Meth
- Crack meth
- Go fast

- Crank
- L.A. glass
- Crystal
- Poor man's coke

PARAPHERNALIA

- Glass pipes
- Cut-off straws
- Hypodermic needles

- Lighters
- Razor blades

PRICES

- Crank sells for $50 to $150 per gram
- Ice sells for $200 to $500 per gram

GLOSSARY

ACUTE
The short term effect of a single dose of drugs.

ANALGESIC
Reduces the sensation of pain (pain relieving).

ANESTHETIC
Reduces all sensation in the body.

"ANGEL DUST"
Slang term for PCP (Phenycyclidine).

"BAG"
Ten (10) to fifteen (15) dollars worth of heroin.

"BINDLE"
Ten (10) to fifteen (15) dollars worth of heroin.

"BLOWING UP"
An expression used when someone is under the influence of ecstasy (MDMA).

"BLUNT"
Marijuana packed in a hollowed out cigar.

"BODY PACKER"
A person who swallows condoms or balloons filled with drugs. This is a common smuggling technique.

"BUNDLE"

Ten (10) bindles or bags of heroin.

CENTRAL NERVOUS SYSTEM

Consists of the brain, brainstem and spinal cord.

CLANDESTINE LABORATORY

Illegal drug manufacturing facilities usually containing chemicals that are dangerous to humans and to the environment.

COCA PASTE

Paste derived from the coca leaf in the process of making cocaine hydrochloride.

COCAINE HYDROCHLORIDE

Most common form of cocaine. Also known as powder cocaine. It is stable and water soluble.

COMA

State of unconsciousness where a person cannot be aroused.

DESIGNER DRUGS (ANALOG)

Synthetic drugs made in clandestine laboratories. Slight changes are made to illegal drugs' chemical structures producing new drugs that are not regulated under the Controlled Substance Act.

"DIME BAG"

Ten dollars ($10) worth of marijuana

"DIME ROCK"

Ten dollars ($10) worth of crack cocaine.

DOSE
The amount of a drug taken.

EUPHORIA
A sense of extreme wellbeing.

"G"
One (1) gram.

HALLUCINOGEN
A drug that produces alteration of one's perception.

"HIT"
Term used for a single dose.

INSOMNIA
Inability to sleep.

JOINT
A marijuana cigarette.

"KEY/KILO"
Kilogram (2.2 pounds)

NATURALLY DERIVED DRUGS
Drugs that are produced from naturally occurring substances.

POLYDRUG USE
When a person takes more than one drug at a time.

PRECURSOR
A chemical that is critical in the manufacturing of a controlled substance.

ROLLING
Term used to indicate ecstasy use.

SEMI-SYNTHETIC DRUGS
Drugs made in laboratories; however, involve some natural substances.

SHAKE
Remaining powder or flakes after cutting large amounts of cocaine.

SYNTHETIC DRUGS
Drugs that are made with precursors and other chemicals in a laboratory. These drugs do not contain any natural substances.

SYNTHESIS
The formation of a chemical compound.

TOLERANCE
The body's natural resistance to the effects of a drug resulting in the increased amount of drugs being consumed to obtain a high.

WITHDRAWAL
The discomfort experienced (physically and/or psychologically) when a person who is addicted to a drug discontinues its use.

About the Author

Detective Scott W. Perkins has been employed by the Orlando Police Department since August 1991. He spent his first year in the Patrol Division and subsequent years with the Drug Enforcement Division. In addition to drug enforcement assignments, Detective Perkins is a member of the Orlando Police Department's SWAT Team. Detective Perkins has conducted extensive undercover operations involving the new wave of Raves and the designer and club drugs associated with them. He was featured on and consulted with ABC's 20/20 and Turning Point on the subjects of Raves, designer drugs and heroin. He also addressed these subjects on two national teleconferences. In 1996 Detective Perkins was named Florida's Narcotic Officer of the Year by the Florida Narcotic Officers' Association. The American Police Hall of Fame & Museum named him Law Enforcement Officer of the Year for 1998 for his role in the successful rescue of two small children who were held hostage for 68 hours by a murder suspect. The Orlando Police Department awarded him the Medal of Valor for his heroic actions and the Purple Heart for the gunshot wound he sustained during the rescue.

Prior to Detective Perkins' career as a police officer, he spent five years in the United States Army. He served as a paratrooper with the 82nd Airborne Division and then as a demolition/engineer sergeant with the Army Special Forces (Green Berets).

Currently Detective Perkins teaches courses throughout the United States to civilian law enforcement and military police on the subjects of Raves, designer and club drugs, undercover drug operations, tactical drug operations, and tactical operations in rural environments.

In addition, he has designed seminars for parents, educators, community leaders and businesses focusing on drug abuse and awareness, Raves, and designer and club drugs.

All data contained in this guide is based upon information we believe is authentic. However, publisher does not assume responsibility for its accuracy.